FREEDOM AND DEMOCRACY

FREEDOM AND DEMOCRACY

LEVEL9/FREE

Contents

WARNING: PLEASE READ	1
ASK YOURSELVES THIS?	3
CLAWING BACK TO LIFE	5
CLUB OF PROCESS FOR PROGRESS	7
COMMON SENSE VS NONSENSE	9
CREATIVE JUICES	11
DEAR LORD	13
FEET	15
FREEDOM AND DEMOCRACY	17
GOD PUT ME HERE (Thank you Lord)	19
GOOD LOOKING OUT	21
GROUNDS FOR COMMUNICATION	23
HATE	25
I'VE BEEN THRU IT	27
IN MEMORY OF ANN (My MOTHER)	29
IT'S THE LORDS DAY (IT'S SUNDAY)	31
IT DOES NOT PAY TO BE IMPATIENT!	33
LIFE AND NEGATIVITY (MIXED UP)	35
LIFE PRESERVER AND A ROPE	37
LUCKY AND BLESSED	39
M.A.G.A.	41
MY PERSONAL THOUGHTS	43
MY WIFE WENT TO JAIL	45
NECESSITY	47
OUR HEALTH	49
RACISM	51
RAIN WILL NOT DAMPEN HER SPIRIT	53
SMALL BLESSINGS	55
SOCIAL MEDIA	57
SPIRITUAL SPRINKLES	59
SPIRITUAL WELL-BEING	61

THE CHOICE IS OURS (FREEDOM OR CHAOS)!	63
THE GOOD, BAD and THE UGLY	65
THE POETIC WAY TO DEMOCRACY	67
THE WAR IN THE U.S.A.	69
WOMEN	71
WOMEN ALONE?!?	73
WHO DOES THIS LAND BELONG TO???	75
WHY?	77

WARNING: PLEASE READ

This is something
that is straight from the heart!

ASK YOURSELVES THIS?

I would like to know
from the bottom of your heart
after living in ongoing bliss
I want you to ask yourselves this:

Am I ready to,
give up the freedom,
I have earned and,
the democracy that is not a sore thumb!

This is a hard question
to ask of oneself
knowing, that, you could not
ask that of anyone else!

These are two things
I ask you to think about
I know in my heart,
those are things I can't do WITHOUT!!

                                                    FREE

CLAWING BACK TO LIFE

Little by little,
I am clawing my way
back to life!

Started off,
meeting someone special
now she is my wife!

They say you have to crawl before you walk!
I am doing things another way so I can talk!

Clawing my way back to a life that I should live!
Speaking to people is the Lords WAY for me to give!

Come a long way,
to be able

to write and mean what I say!

I've had a long road to get where I am at right now!

Well worth it though,
I just you should KNOW!

GOD LEAD THE WAY!!!
FREE

CLUB OF PROCESS FOR PROGRESS

We belong to this club,
whether we like it or not!
Who wants to be apart of life
feeling like progress is about to stop!

Now, when you put in an application,
the company, will do a background check
from the owner, managers, will have a say in,
if you get the job or claim you're a wreck!

Since we are the primary owners of
the United States, who we hire,
is our choice, by voting,
we make decisions on who to fire!

There is a process,

when it comes down to our progress
look at what we have to go through
just to start the process!

                                                        FREE

P.S. (what if you could avoid background checks)!!!

COMMON SENSE VS NONSENSE

Flip a coin,
heads is common sense,
tails its nonsense
which side are you wanting!

The pick between the sides
can be awfully daunting,
choosing the wrong side
could be very haunting!

It is a sad thought,
knowing we have two parties
and only one of them works
for American rights and principals!

Just think,
if both of them,
were doing they're jobs,
we would be back to invincible!

FREE

CREATIVE JUICES

I'm just letting them flow
I've always had creativity within me
being able to convey my point to those
who might have an artistic degree!

One thing for sure is
I will not back away from
a person who wants to throw shade.
I did earn my right to try and persuade!

We all have creative ideas
some of us can't be as creative
as others may,
but that does not mean we don't have
something to say!

Maybe we all could learn
a thing or two,
by listening,
to me or you!

FREE

DEAR LORD

Thank you,
For always being there for me!
Bringing me out of some of the toughest times!
Looking out for me, when I had no idea you were right by my side!
Thank you for blessing me the way you have !
You have bestowed all the things one could ask for!
Even if we thought that it is a difficult situation we have been in, you are there to bail us out!

THANK YOU DEAR LORD!!!

FREE
(much love)

FEET

Finally, workin' on them,
three years in the making,
so unstable, a lot of pain,
One thing I was not faking!

Out of need,
I had to rest my feet
after the foot clinic,
well I was put to sleep!

Don't be laughing at me;
after trying every sport,
as old as I am now
I want my feet for support!

All this time,
the worst thing
would happen to me,
feet please let me be!

FREE

FREEDOM AND DEMOCRACY

I LOVE THE FREEDOM I HAVE!

I REALLY ENJOY THE DEMOCRACY!!
WHAT ABOUT YOU ALL?
WHAT COULD BE BETTER THAN THIS?

FREE
(BESIDES GOING TO HEAVEN)

GOD PUT ME HERE (Thank you Lord)

I know,
deep down inside,
that in GODS heart
is where I reside!

This is an appealing
aspect in my life
because all this time
he helps me overcome strife!

Every stage through my life journey
he has always been in my heart
one thing I know for sure
he is one SPIRIT from who I'll never depart!

FREE

GOOD LOOKING OUT

Back in the day,
we had a way
of thanking each other,
using words that turned out a positive way!

GOOD LOOKING OUT!

Knowing we, are in a pickle
from my point of view,
I write these things because,
GOD is looking out too!

As people of the United States
there are times, we,
as human beings,
need help making up our mind!

Right now,
in this time and space,
a decision to be made
about the human race!

GOOD LOOKING OUT!!

FREE

GROUNDS FOR COMMUNICATION

If it is one thing
we will not do,
it is sitting down
and talking things through!

Bad stuff happens in life,
that is grounds for communication,
just to ease ones strife!

Talking over problems
is one way to resolve them!

We here in the United States
are able to find
grounds for communication,

looking forward to freedom and democracy,
which are stabilizers of our NATION!

FREE

HATE

Is this even a cool
thing to discuss!
Because living with one
another, we build trust!

Having that keeps us
caring for each other!
The LORD put us here
like sister and brother!

We have one of the most
engaging, yet loving,
country, yet to be matched
that only attracts wonderful people!

How and why should
we go wrong,
if you look at it
it is the only place we belong!!

FREE

I'VE BEEN THRU IT

Well, here I go,
just letting you know,
I've been thru it before!

If I could do it all,
over again,
I'd make sure that
there would be a win!

Can't say life was all that great
young as I was
I just would not wait!

I will not bore you
with things I've been thru,

but, making better decisions
is best for YOU!!

FREE

IN MEMORY OF ANN (My MOTHER)

For as long
as I can remember,
my MOTHER taught me from
when I was born,to the month of SEPTEMBER!

I know what I know
because she took the time out,
to show her little boy,
what LIFE was going to be ABOUT!

Along with the LORD,
she always motivated me
to overcome the odds,
and become, the best I could BE!!!!

WITH the help of GOD,

And my lovely WIFE
learning from her
has helped me overcome,
and move on with my LIFE!!

FREE

IT'S THE LORDS DAY (IT'S SUNDAY)

Well, she has now departed,
the spiritual LOVE,
within her,
has just started!

THE LOVE FROM GOD KEEPS ME MOTIVATED!!

The need of us obeying mans laws
keeps me thinking I should take a pause!
I must keep my mind,
on this justifiable cause!

There is thing we have going for us
the line printed on money;

IN GOD WE TRUST!!!

THE things we know are right
we tend to forget about them,
OVERNIGHT!!!

WE HAVE TOO MUCH TO LOSE WHEN WE KNOW
THAT THE LORD HAS BLESSED US
WITH THE THINGS WE HAVE NOW!!!!

                                                          FREE

WE HAVE A MYSTERIOUS GOD!!!!
THANK YOU!

                                                          AMEN

IT DOES NOT PAY TO BE IMPATIENT!

Well I have been patient enough
it is time for me,
to finally get tough!

If you are anything like me,
it is a day late,
and a dollar short!

When it comes to money,
I just can't wait!
It should be here
straight out the gate!

No patience at all
I lose it so quick,
without money, I start to fall!

FREE

LIFE AND NEGATIVITY (MIXED UP)

Lately, life has been really negative,
seems like it is all mixed up!
Why you ask? I can't figure it out
maybe listening to negativity
is what it's all about!

I have always been able to look at things
with a positive point of view, but now,
it's alright to stay positive, despite wrong things
trying to figure it out and how!

You can't stop listening to
people who say just about anything
one person's point of view,
depends on the positivity they can bring!

Let me tell it,
what one says, makes me stop and wonder;
is hearing one speak
turns out to be a total blunder!

Life to me, has been full of mistakes,
I have gotten up, dusted myself off,
jumped back into the ring of life
and be ready, even if there is another loss!

FREE

HANG IN THERE

LIFE PRESERVER AND A ROPE

I was drowning in the sea of love
trying my best to come up in the world!
Boy, let me tell you about the way I felt
out there in the middle, rolling like a whale!

If it was not for the LORD,
who in his wise way, I as of this moment,
might not have a place to stay!

Being on your own, from 14 to 68
is not something,
one can say is great!

I have been at this a long time
just now able to use my mind!
(what little I have left of it)!

Along comes the LORD
blessed me with SHERRI,
the life preserver and a rope,
since then my life has been MERRY!

FREE

LUCKY AND BLESSED

Lucky, for real,
man, you all don't know
how I really feel!

Blessed, so much I can only feel
that I know in my heart
it's got to be GOD'S will!

What else am I supposed to say,
what else am I to say,
I don't want GOD,
to stop sending blessings my way!

FREE

M.A.G.A.

We are a nation of immigrants
so, what is the problem!!
Others have come and made their way
why are we not greeting people,
that want to fit in!!!

Make America greet again
were we invited in graciously
I think it is only proper,
to invite those in need!!!

Our doors have always been open
why should we start closing them now
We need to make America greet again
you all just need to figure out HOW!!!

FREE

MY PERSONAL THOUGHTS

Had to start over;

The devil has come to break down
what the LORD has kept together!

All these years, bloodshed, striving
to keep everlasting love forever!

Are we really willing to give up on ourselves
and abandon the things we find disgusting!

We as a country,
need to wake up and smell the coffee
let alone keep our dignity,
and show we appreciate our DEMOCRACY!!!

WE as the UNITED STATES OF AMERICA
have always overcome our problems
what we always do is,
come together and SOLVE THEM!!!

(WE HAVE THE LOVE OF GOD,
LET ALONE OURSELVES
TO COUNT ON)!!!!

FREE

MY WIFE WENT TO JAIL

What for?
What she do?
Not a thing!
GOD asked her!

I think she is spreading his word!
Whenever HE ask,
She right there
to accept his reward!

One thing I am glad about is she is keeping her obligation to
the LORD!!!

It is necessary for each person
to keep a relationship with the HOLY one!
We all will need him

before our life is done!

Remember, if it weren't for him we would not EXIST!!!

I envy her
for how she is so faithful!
That is one trait
that keeps her beautiful!!!

(She was not put in a cell)

FREE

NECESSITY

These things I write out of necessity;
We must maintain our democracy!
Internal determination is within us
knowing the Lord, builds up our trust!

Only Americans will be the ones,
to make sure the important things get done!
Decisions come to us,
and we make positive moves as one!

Nobody understands us better than
the Lord, we are the only ones who come close,
to living the way he meant for us to live
now it is our turn to appreciate,
from his heart to us he did give!

OUT OF NECESSITY,IS WHY HE IS ALWAYS WITH US!!!

FREE

OUR HEALTH

We have to establish
a mental toughness
that, we probably have never
had to use, still
there is no excuse!

As of this time,
my health is not
to my liking.(I am old)!

Just make sure you are healthy enough to VOTE!!

FREE

RACISM

This can be a bitter but,
necessary subject to discuss!
With it being about Americans,
who better can talk about it than us!

Is it a component of our democracy?
Only if we allow it to be!

It is an internal thing,
built on ones on thoughts!

Do we have to be racist
to be a democracy?

Personally I do not think so!
With it, I think it stunts our growth!

These are my thoughts on racism,
after choosing to become an educated individual!
It is up to each person, to want to become a
really true American!

FREE

SPEAK ON IT!!!

RAIN WILL NOT DAMPEN HER SPIRIT

As the rain
was coming down,
she headed out the door
knowing she might drown!

From working,
at the post office,
to spreading the LORDS WORD,
she makes sure it's delivered
from curb to curb!

The LORD she worships
is a protector of his flock
that is why, spiritually
she just can not be stopped!

ONE OF THE LORDS WARRIORS!!!

SMALL BLESSINGS

GOD, you of all,
the LORD of LORDS,
has always dropped, small blessings,
to shower us with REWARDS!

Thanks pour out of my heart
for all you have bestowed us with,
the small blessings, from you,
have fulfilled our every wish!

Small Blessing,
is finding a friend,
after 30 years!

Being able to
communicate about

any and everything!

Showing the true
meaning of for
better or worse!

Finding a spouse
that you can do
life with!

Finding Love

SHERRI@FREE

SOCIAL MEDIA

This is as close as,
I am going to come to SOCIAL MEDIA!

I have to create my own
way to socialize with others.
My thought process is to,
talk to people like they are my brothers!

Never is it easy,
to always get folks to see things your way
I feel that we should be able,
to discuss things, just listen what we have to say!

It is a necessary understanding
to speak with one another in a diplomatic setting
so we will not say things we'll be regretting!

I am own my best behavior
as long as I write with the
encouragement of my Savior!

This is my social media!

FREE

SPIRITUAL SPRINKLES

Even though,
there was still moisture
in the air
GOD'S spirit was everywhere!

My journey, throughout life,
has been filled with
the LORD,
helping me to overcome strife!

Whenever she is on her way
to church,
that is when I know
the LORD is at work!

One can feel,
a certain way,
but, we all can feel
the LOVE of GOD EVERY DAY!!

FREE

SPIRITUAL WELL-BEING

This is one thing
we all must work on!
It is the most important aspects
to be beside him as he sits on the throne!

If we get back to the basics
of our spiritual well-being,
a lot of things, as humans,
hopefully,GOD will intervene!

I grew up in the Church
as most of us have,
even though it was a non-denominational church,
our spiritual well-being was one thing we had!

Just think, as a nation,
how easy the decisions we have to make,
would be knowing,
we had GOD to thank!

FREE

THE CHOICE IS OURS (FREEDOM OR CHAOS)!

I must be,
someone who is really, really kind;
I keep on writing things to you,
that are very, very relaxing to your mind!

We all have forgotten,
about the freedom that defines us!
Why would we want a world
full of chaos and mistrust?!

Deep down inside,
we deserve better than that
but, if we make a mistake
it is what we will be looking at!

It has been such a long time
experiencing this freedom which is such a blessing
I know of no other way, to keep my mind free
and continue life without the thought of stressing!!

FREE

THE GOOD, BAD and THE UGLY

This is a small summary of my life: Woe is me!

A a youngster
moms would send me
along with my dad
on his afternoon ride.

As we were making our
way back home, he would always say
don't tell your momma nothing,
well, I had to say something!

That is when my problems
with him started.
The good part of my early life
was going to church, after that, we parted!

What happened,
well, according to him,
the house got to small, for both of us
one of us was going to have to leave;
knowing I paid no bills,I kicked dust!

I have no ill will towards anyone,
that part of my life is over and I,
have moved on,
writing for other people, lets me know,
that I am really strong!

WITH THE LORDS HELP!
(of course)!!!

                                              FREE

THE POETIC WAY TO DEMOCRACY

There are more thoughtful ways
to bring about positive ground
for us to work together on!
This is the way Christ was born!

I am saying these things,
to help us reach a goal!
As Americans, together,
we should have one soul!

This is a poetic way
to express our inner thoughts
in a moral, yet, ethical reality
only the LORD has taught!

This is my way
of letting everyone know
we have only us,
to help us GROW!

FREE

THE WAR IN THE U.S.A.

It is a bad thing
for us to be fighting an
internal war every day,
but, a war in the USA!!!

Seems to me, we dispute everything!

Are we a Democracy?

That decision will be answered shortly!

It needs to be put to bed as soon as possible!

Just to make sense of it all
we must have common ground,

if there is a dispute,
pinpoint it, then together,
there will be something we can work around!!!

FREE

WOMEN

One place I do not agree
with MEN on;
is taking away a woman's right,
doing that will keep us up all night!

What made men pick on the WOMEN?

We can not exist
without a woman
toting us around
for nine months!

What were men thinking
deciding abortion was illegal!
Did anybody ask them or,
was you all drunk!

I have to much love and respect for them!
How they feel is the important thought;
Not a politician who, in the long run,
was probably bought!

FREE
(I wrote it!)

WOMEN ALONE?!?

For the life of me
there is one thing I don't understand,
why we took freedoms away from women?

The Lord said we do not need seek revenge
but, in this case, the women will
hang men out to dry!

While we are hanging there
I figure, being out there
we will break down and cry!

Women, who went 9 months,
carried us through all the pain
it took to carry us, deserve better!

I ENVY my mother, knowing she had me,
raised me, sacrificed her freedom,
to make sure I had mine!

OF ALL THE CRAZY THINGS A MAN COULD DO!!
WHY TAKE FREEDOM FROM THEM
WHEN IT DOES NOT BELONG TO YOU!!!

FREE

WHO DOES THIS LAND BELONG TO???

GOD!!!

He gave it to us
hoping we would
prosper from it!

The way I see IT, we should make the necessary decision,
who our **PRESIDENT** is!!!

FREE

WHY?

Why!
Do we have an answer?
First; What is the question?

Well! #1; Why are we in the situation we are in?
Does anyone have an answer?
How about believing the wrong words
are truthful!

#2; How do we fix it?
We go to the LORD!
He has always had the answer
to all of our Prayers!

If a person has so much to say about the
way things are, then maybe they should

do something positive to help!!

ME, I love it in the United States,
we are from all different backgrounds!
And we have fought long and hard to
keep the blessings around!

#3; Should we give up now?
I do not think the LORD would allow that!
Would you?
Could you?

#4; Are we not the beacon for the rest of Humanity?
Maybe now is the time to get our act
together!
Lets do this, spread the love,
lets live like this FOREVER!!!

FREE

Made in the USA
Coppell, TX
23 May 2025

49816322R00049